Greatest COMEBACKS in Sports

by

Dustin Long

Published by ABDO Publishing Company, PO Box 398166, Minneapolis, MN 55439. Copyright © 2014 by Abdo Consulting Group, Inc. International copyrights reserved in all countries. No part of this book may be reproduced in any form without written permission from the publisher. SportsZone™ is a trademark and logo of ABDO Publishing Company.

Printed in the United States of America,
North Mankato, Minnesota
052013
112013

Editor: Chrös McDougall
Series Designer: Craig Hinton

Photo Credits: L.M. Otero/AP Images, cover, 1, 31; AP Images, 5, 35, 44, 51, 53, 58; Denis Peroy/AP Images, 8; Mark Humphrey/AP Images, 11; Charles Krupa/AP Images, 13; Amy Sancetta/AP Images, 15; Ray Stubblebine/AP Images, 18; Eric Gay/AP Images, 20; Greg Trott/AP Images, 23; Houston Chronicle, Dave Einsel/AP Images, 26; Scott Audette/AP Images, 29; Bill Kostroun/AP Images, 32; Danny Johnston/AP Images, 37; Carl Viti/AP Images, 39; Robert Stinnett/Oakland/Tribune/AP Images, 40; Matt York/AP Images, 43; Amy E. Conn/AP Images, 47; Pete Leabo/AP Images, 48; Kevork Djansezian/AP Images, 55; Ed Bailey/AP Images, 56

Library of Congress Control Number: 2013932659

Cataloging-in-Publication Data
Long, Dustin.
 Greatest comebacks in sports / Dustin Long.
  p. cm. -- (Sports' biggest moments)
ISBN 978-1-61783-924-5
Includes bibliographical references and index.
1. Sports comebacks--Juvenile literature. 2. Sports--Miscellanea--Juvenile literature. I. Title.
796--dc23

                                    2013932659

TABLE OF CONTENTS

Chapter 1

GREAT COLLEGE BASKETBALL COMEBACKS

O nly 17 seconds remained. The University of North Carolina Tar Heels trailed the archrival Duke University Blue Devils by eight points. All seemed lost for North Carolina and its fans.

Today a team could forge a comeback using three long baskets. But this was 1974. The three-point line would not become part of college basketball for years. So North Carolina's only hope was to rally the old-fashioned way.

The Tar Heels had made a dramatic comeback two months earlier against Duke. That time North Carolina hit a last-second shot to win the game. But a comeback this time appeared very unlikely. Not only would the Tar Heels need eight points, but they would need to score those eight points in 17 seconds.

Dean Smith led the Tar Heels to 879 wins in his career, but perhaps none was as dramatic as the 1974 game against Duke.

Yet against the odds, North Carolina rallied. Forward Bobby Jones got things started when he hit two free throws. That cut Duke's lead to 86–80 without any time coming off the clock. Then forward Walter Davis intercepted Duke's inbound pass and threw the ball to teammate John Kuester. He hit a layup. Duke's lead dwindled to 86–82 with 13 seconds left.

Hope began to build among North Carolina fans. Then Duke lost the ball again. Davis missed a shot, but Jones snatched the rebound and scored. North Carolina now trailed 86–84 with six seconds left. The crowd at North Carolina's Carmichael Auditorium jumped, screamed, and cheered. Suddenly victory didn't feel so far away.

The Tar Heels fouled to stop the clock. That gave Duke a chance to extend its lead to two possessions. But the Blue Devils missed a free throw and a North Carolina player grabbed the rebound. The Tar Heels called a time out with three seconds remaining. They would have to go the length of the court and put up a shot to tie the game. Even then that would only force overtime. The odds were still against North Carolina.

"The whole time the comeback was happening, coach [Dean] Smith was very calm in the huddle," North Carolina forward Ed Stahl said. "He had an uncanny confidence in those situations. He would always say something like, 'Isn't this fun?' And it was. When we broke the huddle, we always had the belief that it would play out the way we had prepared for it to."

Smith drew up a play for Davis to get the ball and fire a shot before the buzzer.

"Coach wanted me to catch the ball at midcourt," Davis said. "I was afraid that if Mitch [Kupchak] had to throw the ball that far, it might be intercepted. So I ran into the backcourt to receive the pass. I took three dribbles and put up a shot. I thought I was close enough that I could try to swish it . . . When it left my hand, I wasn't sure that it was good."

Davis's shot from approximately 30 feet didn't swish. It banked into the basket before the buzzer, sending fans rushing onto the court in celebration. The fans had to return to their seats. But they soon had reason to celebrate more. North Carolina clinched the 96–92 victory in overtime.

North Carolina's comeback was so improbable that Smith had his players run the game-tying play again the next day in practice. This time Davis missed the shot. But it didn't matter. When it counted, Davis hit the shot that capped off one of the greatest comebacks in college basketball history.

UNLV's Curtis Terry shoots a three-pointer at the buzzer in regulation to tie San Diego State in their 2005 game.

Making a Name for Himself

Curtis Terry was a freshman at the University of Nevada-Las Vegas (UNLV) in 2005, but most knew him as the younger brother of National Basketball Association (NBA) player Jason Terry. That changed when Curtis helped UNLV rally from 10 points down with 18 seconds left against San Diego State University in a regular-season game. Everyone knew who he was then.

Terry completed UNLV's improbable rally by hitting an off-balance three-point shot from the right wing at the buzzer to send the game into overtime. UNLV would go on to win. No other college basketball team has trailed by as many points with as little time left and won.

"I've been coaching and playing for 35 years, and I don't think I've seen a comeback like that," UNLV coach Lon Kruger said after the game.

Super Mario

Fans of the University of Memphis Tigers could practically taste their team's first national championship. Only 2:12 remained in the 2008 national title game, and Memphis led the University of Kansas Jayhawks by nine points. It was only a matter of time before the celebration could begin.

Then momentum changed. Kansas started hitting shots. Meanwhile, Memphis began missing free throws. The Tigers missed four of five free-throw attempts as the Jayhawks pulled to within three points. Now 10 seconds remained and Kansas had the ball.

Kansas guard Mario Chalmers caught a pass on the right wing with five seconds left. He dribbled once to his left. Then he turned toward the basket. Time seemed to stop as Chalmers jumped and put up a shot. A Memphis defender raised his hand. It didn't distract Chalmers. *Swish*. The game was tied with two seconds left.

"Unbelievable!" CBS announcer Jim Nantz shouted.

The national championship game was headed for overtime.

"It'll probably be the biggest shot ever made in Kansas history," Jayhawks coach Bill Self said after the game.

Kansas scored the first six points in overtime. Memphis could get no closer than three points and lost 75–68. The rally gave Kansas its first

Kansas guard Mario Chalmers shoots the three-pointer that sent his Jayhawks into overtime in the 2008 national title game.

national championship in men's basketball in 20 years. For Memphis coach John Calipari, it was not so memorable.

"I have never looked at that [video] tape," Calipari, now coaching the University of Kentucky Wildcats, told reporters in 2012. "That tape was flung out the door of the bus as we were going to the plane [to return home]. So I have never looked at that tape, nor will I."

Chapter 2

GREAT MLB COMEBACKS

No team in Major League Baseball (MLB) had ever lost the first three games of a seven-game playoff series and gone on to win. But in the 2004 American League (AL) Championship Series, the Boston Red Sox set out to do just that. And they would have to do it against their longtime archrivals, the New York Yankees.

For years the Yankees tormented the Red Sox. Boston fans blamed it on the "Curse of the Bambino." That was a supposed curse put on the Red Sox when they sold Babe "The Bambino" Ruth to the Yankees after the 1919 season. The Red Sox had won five World Series before then and the Yankees none. Since, the Yankees had won 26 while Boston had zero.

Yankees fans loved tormenting Red Sox fans. Now they couldn't wait to end another fruitless Red Sox season. Not so fast.

Few people outside of Boston believed in the Red Sox after they went down 3–0 in the 2004 ALCS.

A message was taped to Boston's clubhouse door: "WE CAN CHANGE HISTORY. BELIEVE IT." And that's what the Red Sox set out to do.

Unfortunately, the Yankees weren't about to lie down. In Game 4, the Yankees took a 4–3 lead into the bottom of the ninth inning. They just needed three outs to end Boston's season. But the Red Sox got a walk. Then pinch runner Dave Roberts stole second. Then he scored on a single to tie it. Three innings later in the 12th, Red Sox slugger David Ortiz blasted a two-run homer over the 380-foot marker in right field to send the series to Game 5.

Game 5 went even longer. Boston needed 14 innings before winning on Ortiz's run-scoring single. That set up an even more dramatic Game 6.

Boston pitcher Curt Schilling had been injured throughout the playoffs. He had a torn tendon sheath in his ankle. That made it very painful to pitch. The team's medical staff devised a new procedure that kept his tendon stable and allowed him to pitch. Blood from his ankle seeped onto his white sock during the game, but he kept pitching.

Boston Red Sox players celebrate after beating the New York Yankees in Game 7 of the 2004 AL Championship Series.

When he left the game, Boston led 4–1. The Red Sox went on to win 4–2. The seven-game series was now tied at three games apiece.

Now it was down to one game. The winner would advance to the World Series. The loser would be done for the year. This one wasn't as dramatic. Boston won 10–3 at Yankee Stadium to complete the comeback.

Then the Red Sox went on to sweep the St. Louis Cardinals to claim Boston's first World Series title since 1918.

"How many times can you honestly say you have a chance to shock the world?" Boston's Kevin Millar asked reporters after eliminating the Yankees. "It might happen once in your life, or it might never happen. But we had a chance and we did it."

Tense Game

Some might call Boston's 2004 comeback revenge for what the Yankees did to the Red Sox in 1978. That time it was the Yankees with an incredible comeback.

Boston had a 14-game lead on New York in the standings on July 20. There were no wild-card playoff berths back then. Only the two division winners in each league made the playoffs. But by mid-summer, the Yankees appeared to be doomed. After all, no team had ever come from 14 games back to make the playoffs.

Then the Yankees began one of the most remarkable comebacks in baseball history. They started winning. They had stretches of 8–1, 10–2, and 21–5. The Red Sox, meanwhile, began losing. They lost nine of 10 beginning July 20. Then they went 3–14 during a stretch. The Yankees caught the Red Sox on September 10 after sweeping a four-game series in Boston. They took over the division lead three days later.

Both teams rallied down the stretch. The Yankees won six in a row before losing the season finale. Up in Boston, an eight-game winning streak to end the regular-season was just enough to tie New York in the standings.

So the two rivals would play one extra game. The winner would go to the playoffs. The loser was done for the season. They met on October 2, 1978, at Boston's Fenway Park.

"That was as much tension as you can have, as intense a game as there ever was," New York's Chris Chambliss recalled 20 years later.

The Red Sox led 2–0 going into the seventh inning. Then Chambliss hit a one-out single for New York. Roy White followed with a hit. An out later, Bucky Dent stepped to the plate. Nobody figured he would give the Yankees the lead. He'd have to hit a home run to do that. He had hit only four all season.

That's what Dent did. He slammed a one-ball, one-strike pitch over the huge left field wall named the Green Monster for a three-run home run. The Yankees led 3–2. They won the game 5–4 and made the playoffs.

The New York Yankees' Bucky Dent hits a three-run homer against the Boston Red Sox in the 1978 divisional playoff game.

The game still haunts Red Sox fans. New York would go on to win the World Series for a second consecutive year. It wouldn't have been possible without Dent's home run.

Destiny's Team

The St. Louis Cardinals weren't supposed to be celebrating a World Series championship in 2011. They weren't even supposed to be in the playoffs.

They were 10.5 games out of a playoff spot with 31 games left in the season. They were still three games out of the playoffs with five games to go. Yet St. Louis rallied to make the playoffs as the wild-card team after winning the regular-season finale.

The momentum continued as the Cardinals marched all the way to the World Series. But the amazing run appeared to be ending in Game 6 against the Texas Rangers. The Cardinals trailed 7–5 with one out remaining in the bottom of the ninth inning. Then David Freese, who grew up in St. Louis as a Cardinals fan, stepped in and took one ball and two strikes.

One more strike and the Rangers would be World Series champs. Instead, Freese hit a two-run triple off the right field wall to tie the game.

DON'T COUNT THEM OUT

The 2012 playoffs featured some of the most memorable comebacks. The St. Louis Cardinals rallied from a 6–0 deficit to defeat the Washington Nationals and clinch their NL Division Series. It was the largest comeback in a series-clinching game in MLB history. Also, the San Francisco Giants became the first team to lose the first two games of a best-of-five series at home and win the next three on the road to clinch a series. The Giants rallied to beat the Cincinnati Reds and later went on to win the World Series.

David Freese meets his St. Louis Cardinals teammates at home plate as he scores the winning run in Game 6 of the 2011 World Series.

Texas quickly put a damper on the celebration by taking a two-run lead in the top of the 10th inning. St. Louis again got down to its last strike in the bottom of the inning. But then Lance Berkman hit a game-tying, line-drive single.

Freese ultimately was the hero. He won the game in the bottom of the 11th inning with a home run over the center field wall.

"What happened today," St. Louis manager Tony La Russa told reporters afterward, "I just think you had to be here to believe it."

St. Louis went on to claim the World Series title with a 6–2 victory the next night.

CLAWING BACK

The Detroit Tigers trailed the St. Louis Cardinals three games to one in the best-of-seven 1968 World Series after losing Games 3 and 4 by a combined score of 17–4. Detroit rallied to win the next three games, beating St. Louis and its best pitcher in Game 7, to become World Series champions.

Chapter 3

GREAT NFL COMEBACKS

Sometimes the greatest comebacks aren't by a team but by a person. Kurt Warner is one such example. The man who led the St. Louis Rams to a Super Bowl victory did not start at quarterback in college until his senior year. No National Football League (NFL) team selected him in the 1994 draft. He joined the Green Bay Packers but was cut in training camp.

Warner returned to his home in Iowa after that. Instead of playing football, he worked at a grocery store. Sometimes his shift ended at 3 o'clock in the morning. Sometimes his shift ended at 7 o'clock in the morning. He stocked shelves. He swept floors. He helped customers load groceries in their cars.

"Talk about a humbling experience," Warner wrote in the book about his life.

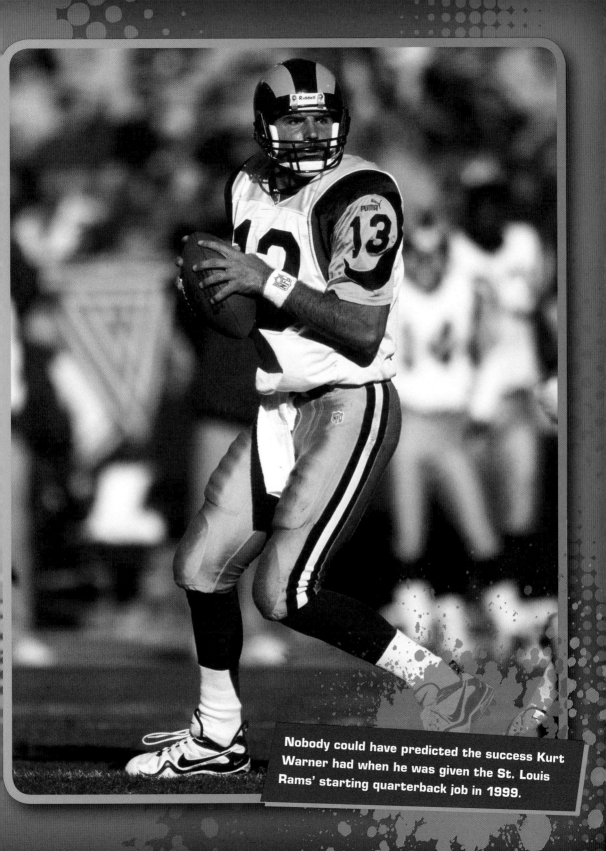

Nobody could have predicted the success Kurt Warner had when he was given the St. Louis Rams' starting quarterback job in 1999.

His football career seemed over, but Warner wouldn't quit. He continued to pursue his dream of playing in the NFL. He played in other leagues. He even played football in Europe. His determination would be rewarded. Three years after being cut by the Packers, Warner signed with the St. Louis Rams. He was back in the NFL.

He played only one game in 1998. It looked like the 1999 season would be the same. Then the Rams' starting quarterback was injured in the preseason. Warner stepped in as St. Louis' starting quarterback.

Fans were disappointed. The Rams had been one of the worst teams in the NFL the year before. Any hopes of improvement seemed to disappear with Warner starting. Warner proved them all wrong. He led an offense so good it became known as "The Greatest Show on Turf." In one year the Rams went from 4–12 and last place in the division to 13–3 and first place. Warner was selected as the NFL's Most Valuable Player (MVP).

BEGINNING OF GREATNESS

It was an ordinary regular-season game in December 1980. That is, until history was made. The San Francisco 49ers trailed the New Orleans Saints by 28 points. Then they came back to win 38–35 in overtime. It was the greatest regular-season comeback in NFL history. The game was also considered a turning point in team history. The 49ers had never experienced much success in prior years. They won their first Super Bowl after the 1981 season. Then they won four more after the 1984, 1988, 1989, and 1994 seasons. That made the 49ers one of the most successful teams in NFL history.

Warner's comeback was not yet complete, though. He guided the Rams all the way to the Super Bowl. The Rams and Tennessee Titans were tied 16–16 with 2:12 left. Then Warner threw a long touchdown pass to give the Rams the lead. Tennessee tried to rally. But the game ended with Tennessee one yard from the game-tying touchdown. The St. Louis Rams were Super Bowl champions. Warner was the Super Bowl's MVP.

"It would have been very easy to feel sorry for myself or become bitter and walk away from my dream, but I believed in my talents and kept battling," Warner wrote in his book.

Twice as Nice

Quarterback Frank Reich has been a part of history twice. In college, he led his University of Maryland Terrapins to what was then the biggest comeback in college football history. Then he led his Buffalo Bills to the greatest comeback in NFL history.

"The great thing about being a part of the greatest comeback is it's such a team-oriented thing," Reich said. "It's not like one guy just takes over. You really do need everyone and everything to click. You take pride in the fact that you were on a team that did something special like that."

The first comeback was in 1984. Reich came off the bench with Maryland down 31–0 against the powerful University of Miami Hurricanes. Yet with Reich guiding the offense, the Terrapins came back to win 42–40.

After college Reich played for the Bills. He was the Bills' backup throughout the 1992 season. But an injury to Jim Kelly moved Reich into

Quarterback Frank Reich and kicker Steve Christie celebrate the Buffalo Bills' 41–38 win over the Houston Oilers in January 1993.

the starting role for a playoff game against the Houston Oilers. It was only Reich's seventh NFL start.

It couldn't have been worse early on. Houston led 35–3 in the third quarter. Then Reich got his comeback started. He rallied his team to four touchdowns in the third quarter. Reich threw three touchdown passes during that run.

CAPTAIN COMEBACK

The Denver Broncos' win against the Cincinnati Bengals in a 2012 regular-season game wasn't the largest comeback, but it was a record-setting one. That game marked the forty-eighth time quarterback Peyton Manning led his team to a fourth-quarter comeback win. Prior to that game he had been tied with former Miami Dolphins quarterback Dan Marino for leading the most comebacks in NFL history.

Buffalo only trailed 35–31 after three quarters. Reich threw a 17-yard touchdown pass to Andre Reed with 3:08 left in the fourth quarter. That gave Buffalo a 38–35 lead. Houston came back and tied the game on a field goal with 12 seconds left in the fourth quarter. But Buffalo won 41–38 in overtime on Steve Christie's 32-yard field goal.

"[Backup quarterback] Gale Gilbert said to me at halftime, 'Hey, you did this in college. You can do it here,'" Reich said. "I remember thinking the same thing I thought that day in Miami—one play at a time. One play at a time."

Fast Comeback

All seemed lost for the Indianapolis Colts. They trailed the Tampa Bay Buccaneers 35–14. Less than four minutes remained in the fourth quarter of their 2003 game. No team had ever come back from such a deficit so late in a game. The Colts, though, did not quit.

The rally started with a touchdown run by running back James Mungro. Then the Colts recovered an onside kick. With 2:29 left, quarterback Peyton Manning connected with wide receiver Marvin Harrison. The 28-yard touchdown pass got the Colts to within 35–28. Then running back Ricky Williams scored on a 1-yard run with 35 seconds left. The game went into overtime.

The Colts had a chance to win in overtime but missed a field goal. However, Tampa Bay was called for a penalty. That gave Indianapolis a

Quarterback Peyton Manning and coach Tony Dungy were all smiles after the Indianapolis Colts' 2003 comeback against Tampa Bay.

second chance to kick a field goal. This time, Mike Vanderjagt made the 29-yard kick to complete Indianapolis' remarkable comeback.

"These guys just never gave up," Indianapolis coach Tony Dungy said.

Chapter 4

GREAT NBA COMEBACKS

R eggie Miller was born with a condition that caused his feet to be pointed to the sides instead of forward. Doctors told his parents that he likely would never walk without help. Miller overcame those early challenges to become an NBA star. He even went on to make the Basketball Hall of Fame. Yet he might be most remembered for what he did in just nine seconds during a 1995 NBA playoff game.

Miller's Indiana Pacers had developed a rivalry with the New York Knicks. The Pacers and the Knicks were among the best teams in the NBA's Eastern Conference during the mid-1990s. They also came from very different parts of the country. Miller loved representing basketball-crazy Indiana against the big-city Knicks. He was often the most intense player on the court during already intense games. That showed during their 1995 playoff series.

Reggie Miller of the Indiana Pacers takes the ball up the court late in Game 1 during the 1995 playoffs against the New York Knicks.

Reggie Miller celebrates after his Indiana Pacers beat the New York Knicks in Game 1 of their 1995 playoff series.

The Knicks led 105–99 with 18.7 seconds left in Game 1. The game was at New York's Madison Square Garden. A Knicks victory to open the series seemed certain. Then Miller let loose.

He hit a three-point shot from the left wing with 16.4 seconds left. Then he stole New York's inbound pass, dribbled back to the three-point line, and shot the ball. It swished through the net. The game was tied with 13.3 seconds to play. Miller had scored six points in five seconds.

"We were shell-shocked," New York's Anthony Mason recalled. "We went numb after his second three. It was like a terrible nightmare that you couldn't wake up from."

After New York failed to score, Miller was fouled. He hit both his free throws to give the Pacers a 107–105 lead with 7.5 seconds left. That gave Miller eight points in nine seconds. The Knicks failed to score after that. The Pacers won the game.

"The Knicks, New York, and Madison Square Garden bring out the best in me," Miller said. "Always has. It lights a fire inside of me. There's nothing I want more than to beat them on their stage, to steal their show. I got great enjoyment from that."

True Heart

The Los Angeles Lakers trailed the Seattle SuperSonics by 29 points in a 1989 playoff game. It didn't matter. Los Angeles rallied to win and sweep the series in the greatest comeback in NBA playoff history.

"The prime and heart [of the team] came out," Lakers' star Earvin "Magic" Johnson told reporters after that game. "We never panicked. We never pointed fingers at each other. We just never quit."

The Lakers began their comeback in the first half. Seattle had a 43–14 lead in the second quarter. Then the Lakers outscored Seattle 22–6 in the final 8:02 of the first half. They still trailed by 11 at halftime, though. The Lakers didn't take the lead until 6:14 left to play in the game.

"The Lakers were a team on a mission," Seattle's Nate McMillan said after the game.

Once the Lakers took the lead, they never trailed. They won 97–95. Seattle's season ended. The Lakers advanced to the next round of the playoffs. They would go on to the NBA Finals for

INSPIRATIONAL COMEBACK

No one knew if Willis Reed would play in Game 7 of the 1970 NBA Finals. The New York Knicks' best player had torn a muscle in his right thigh earlier in the series against the Los Angeles Lakers. The injury forced him to miss Game 6. But just before tip-off of Game 7, Reed limped on to the court. The fans roared. His presence inspired the Knicks to win the game and become NBA champions.

Willis Reed, *shown in 1973,* fought through injury to help his New York Knicks beat the Los Angeles Lakers in the 1970 NBA Finals.

the seventh time in eight years. However, they lost to the Detroit Pistons in the championship series.

Clipping the Grizzlies

The second greatest comeback in an NBA playoff game also included a team from Los Angeles. This time it was the Clippers instead of the Lakers. The Los Angeles Clippers trailed the Memphis Grizzlies by 27 points in a 2012 playoff game and won 99–98.

It didn't seem as if the Clippers had a chance in the opening game of their first-round matchup. Memphis was still ahead by 24 with 9:13 left in the game. Clippers coach Vinny Del Negro was about a minute away from pulling his starters and giving up in that game.

Then Los Angeles started making baskets. Memphis missed 12 shots in a row and committed four turnovers. The Grizzlies' lead shrunk. Finally, the Clippers were in the lead. They never let it go.

"I don't remember what happened," Clippers point guard Chris Paul told reporters after the game. "It's all a blur."

A TALE FOR THE GRANDCHILDREN

The Utah Jazz trailed the Denver Nuggets by 36 points on November 27, 1996, and won. It remained the greatest comeback in NBA history through 2012. "I don't like to gloat in the glory," Utah's Karl Malone said afterward, "but that was unbelievable." His teammate Bryon Russell said: "I'm going to remember this and talk about this to my grandchildren." Utah wouldn't give up despite the deficit. Utah outscored Denver in the second half 71–33 to win the game 107–103.

Los Angeles Clippers guard Chris Paul dribbles past Memphis Grizzlies guard Mike Conley during Game 1 of their 2012 playoff series.

The Clippers would go on to win the series in seven games. It was only the third time in the team's history that it won a playoff series. If not for that comeback in Game 1, the Clippers wouldn't have won the series.

Clippers forward Reggie Evans said the Game 1 rally reminded him of another great comeback in NBA history.

"You think about games with the New York Knicks and Reggie Miller and the Indiana Pacers and how they came back and surprised the world," Evans said. "So we just kind of put that swagger back in the game."

Chapter 5

GREAT COLLEGE FOOTBALL COMEBACKS

The situation was desperate for the University of California Golden Bears football team. The archrival Stanford University Cardinal had kicked a field goal and led 20–19 in their November 1982 game. Only four seconds remained. California was having just an average season. But a Stanford victory would send the Cardinal to a bowl game for only the fifth time since 1952. Stanford players celebrated on the sideline.

There was only enough time for the kickoff. California would have to return the kickoff for a touchdown to win the game and end Stanford's season short of a bowl game. The odds were against that happening.

"After Stanford's field goal, I had this really strong feeling it's not over," California's Richard Rodgers told *Sports Illustrated* 30 years after that game.

What happened next became college football lore. Most people now simply refer to it as "The Play."

Members of the Stanford band rush onto the field to celebrate what they thought was a victory over archrival California in 1982.

Surrounded by members of the Stanford band, California's Kevin Moen (26) leaps into the air after scoring his team's winning touchdown.

Kevin Moen fielded the short kickoff at the California 45-yard line. He ran three yards and pitched the ball to his left to Rodgers, his teammate. The bizarre play was under way.

The third California player to touch the ball on the return was nearly tackled. He managed to lateral to a teammate. But some thought the play was over. Stanford's players—and its band—started to rush on to the field. They thought the game had ended and they had won.

Reflected Stanford coach Paul Wiggin, "What could I see? I saw the band, I saw our team, I saw a lateral, I saw a flag go down, I saw a guy pick up a flag, I saw all kinds of things. It was basically a 10-second nightmare."

But the play was still going. Rodgers got the ball back and pitched to a teammate. He lateraled it back to Moen, who caught the ball at the Stanford 24-yard line. Moen ran by two Stanford defenders and charged through the Stanford band for a touchdown. Moen crashed into Gary Tyrrell, a trombone player in the Stanford band, in the end zone.

A great comeback and a marriage proposal? Now that is noteworthy. It was the 2007 Fiesta Bowl. Boise State University was a heavy underdog to the University of Oklahoma. Yet, Boise State had a 28–10 lead in the third quarter. Then Oklahoma rallied. The Sooners tied the game on a two-point conversion with 1:26 left. Then they scored the go-ahead touchdown on an interception with just over a minute left. But Boise tied the game 35–35 with seven seconds to go. Oklahoma again took a seven-point lead in overtime. Boise State also scored a touchdown. An extra point would have tied the game again. But Boise State went for the two-point conversion and the win. Ian Johnson scored on a trick play—the Statue of Liberty—to give Boise State the victory. Afterward, Johnson got down on one knee and proposed to his cheerleader girlfriend on national TV. She said yes.

No one knew if the touchdown would count because so many people were on the field during the play. The referees huddled. Finally, they signaled touchdown for California. The play counted. California had won the game. Stanford lost and would not go to a bowl game.

Moen told *Sports Illustrated* that California used to practice a similar play. The players would try lateraling the ball as often as possible without getting tackled. Such practice proved critical in those final seconds.

It started with a kickoff. It featured several laterals. It ended with a California player running through the Stanford marching band for the game-winning touchdown. The deficit was only one point. But it's easy to see why this is among the greatest comebacks in college football.

Joe Starkey, the California radio broadcaster, screamed into his microphone: "The Bears have won! The Bears have won! The Bears have won! Oh my God, the most amazing, sensational, traumatic, heart-rending . . . exciting, thrilling finish in the history of college football!"

Boise State running back Ian Johnson runs for the winning two-point conversion in overtime of the 2007 Fiesta Bowl.

Tie = Win

Sometimes the greatest comebacks don't always determine a winner.
It was that way when the Harvard University Crimson and the Yale
University Bulldogs played to a 29–29 tie in 1968.

Yale's Calvin Hill (30) battles with two Harvard defenders for a pass during their famous 1968 game in Cambridge, Massachusetts.

The two Ivy League rivals entered undefeated. It was the first time since 1909 that neither had a loss heading into the final game of the season. Yale led Harvard 29–13 with less than a minute left. The Bulldogs appeared headed for their seventeenth consecutive win overall. Then the incredible happened.

Harvard's backup quarterback Frank Champi threw a touchdown pass with 42 seconds left. The two-point conversion play failed. But Yale was called for a penalty. Harvard got a second chance, and this time it converted. Yale's lead was down to 29–21. But Harvard had to get the ball back on the ensuing onside kick or the game would be over.

Harvard indeed recovered the kick. Then the Crimson drove downfield until Champi was sacked on the Yale 8-yard line. Only four seconds remained. There was time for just one last play. Champi dropped back to pass but was pressured and began scrambling. He was looking for any teammate to throw to. Yale defenders pursued. Champi broke one tackle and tossed the ball to the end zone as a Yale defender hit him.

Victor Gatto caught Champi's pass for touchdown to make the score 29–27. There was no time left. The Crimson would need a two-point conversion to avoid the loss. Harvard made the conversion, and the game ended in a 29–29 tie. Harvard fans rushed on to the field to celebrate the tie. Considering the remarkable comeback, many saw the tie as a Harvard win. The *Harvard Crimson*, the school newspaper, ran a banner headline that read, "Harvard Beats Yale 29–29."

Chicken Soup to the Rescue

Sometimes it takes more than one attempt to cap a remarkable comeback. That was the case for the University of Notre Dame in the 1979 Cotton Bowl. The game was played during the most severe storm in Dallas in 30 years. Temperatures were in the low 20s. Wind gusts topped 30 miles per hour (48 km/h). It was bitterly cold.

Notre Dame trailed the University of Houston 34–12 in the third quarter. Notre Dame quarterback Joe Montana spent part of the game in the locker room because of the flu. While in the locker room, Montana ate chicken soup. He soon returned to the game, and magic happened.

First Notre Dame blocked a punt and ran it back for a touchdown. Then the Fighting Irish added the two-point conversion with 7:25 left. Montana ended the next drive by running for a touchdown. Now Notre Dame trailed 34–28 with 4:15 left. Notre Dame got the ball back with less than a minute left. It had one last chance to win the game.

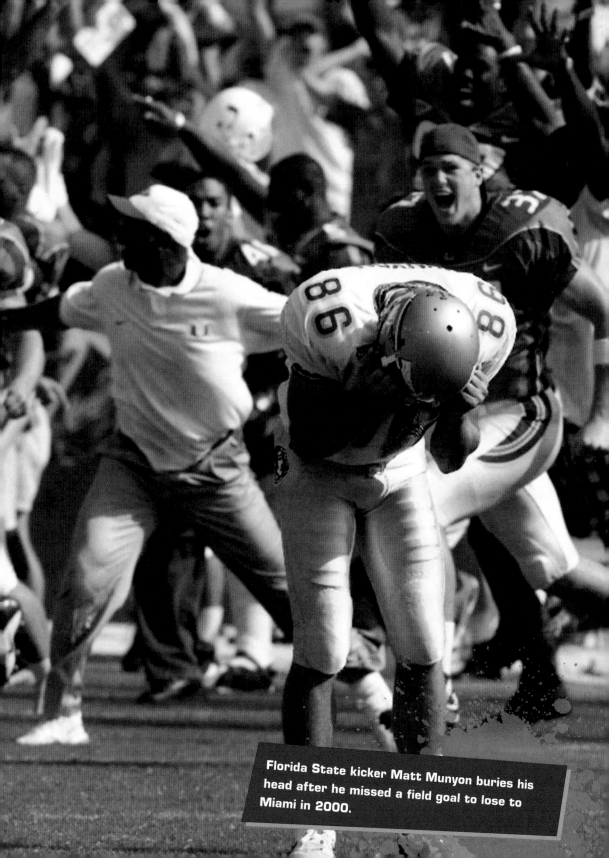

Florida State kicker Matt Munyon buries his head after he missed a field goal to lose to Miami in 2000.

Notre Dame split end Kris Haines celebrates after catching the game-tying touchdown against Houston in the 1979 Cotton Bowl.

WE ARE MARSHALL

One of the greatest comebacks in college football took years to accomplish. A plane carrying the Marshall football team crashed on November 14, 1970. All 75 people on the plane, including players and coaches, died. The football team would have to be rebuilt. The movie *We Are Marshall* was based on that first season after the plane crash. It would take Marshall 14 seasons to have a winning season. Twenty-two years after the plane crash, Marshall won the Division I-AA national championship, completing its comeback.

On the frozen field, Montana avoided a Houston defender and rolled right. He completed an 8-yard touchdown pass to a diving Kris Haines to tie the game with no time left. Notre Dame only needed to make the extra-point kick to complete this stunning rally.

And Joe Unis made the kick. Wait—there was a penalty. It was against Notre Dame. Unis had to do the extra-point kick again from farther away. He made it again, and this time it counted. Led by its sick quarterback, Notre Dame had come from behind to win the bowl game, 35–34.

Chapter 6

MORE GREAT COMEBACKS

The greatest comebacks often occur when all appears hopeless for an athlete or a team. That was the case for Lasse Viren, a runner from Finland, at the 1972 Olympic Games in Munich, Germany.

Viren was a village policeman who trained for years to run in the Olympic Games. He was running fifth halfway through the 10,000-meter Olympic race when another runner accidentally bumped him. Viren fell to the track. The crowd gasped. The leaders pulled away as Viren picked himself off the ground.

His chance for a gold medal seemed lost. All that training seemed wasted. But Viren wouldn't give up. He couldn't.

The crowd cheered as Viren got back up. He had lost approximately 25 meters on the others. Yet within one lap of the 400-meter track he had raced back and caught the pack. But had he used up too much energy to

Finland's Lasse Viren (228) battles for position in the 10,000-meter race at the 1972 Olympic Games in Munich, West Germany.

catch the leaders? Would he be strong enough to make a move at the end of the race? Or would he not be able to maintain the pace the leaders set?

The 10,000-meter race is a grueling 25 laps around the track. Viren had fallen on lap 12. But he hung in the pack. He made his move with 600 meters left. That is one-and-a-half laps around the track. It would take an amazing effort to keep his speed up for that long.

Viren was in the lead. He remained there as the runners began the final lap. This would determine who would win the gold medal.

Viren began to pull away from the other runners. Gold looked as if it would be his. With about a quarter-lap left in the race, the crowd buzzed with excitement. The runner in second place was gaining on Viren. The gap between Viren and the second-place runner was only a couple of feet as they made the turn out of the final corner. Just one straightaway to go for the gold medal.

Could Viren hold on to the lead and overcome his early fall? Suddenly, Viren shot forward with a burst of speed. He pulled away.

"DON'T WORRY"

The Toronto Maple Leafs trailed the Detroit Red Wings in the 1942 Stanley Cup Finals three games to none. Toronto had to win all four remaining games to win the title. Toronto's Billy Taylor wasn't worried. He told the press before Game 4: "Don't worry about us, we'll beat them four straight." That's what they did. Through 2012, Toronto remained the only team in National Hockey League (NHL) history to come back from a 3–0 deficit in a seven-game series to win the Stanley Cup.

Viren crossed the finish line first to win the gold medal. And not only that, he also set a world record despite falling earlier in the race. Viren's comeback is regarded among the greatest comebacks in Olympic history. He followed it up by winning the 5,000-meter race ten days later.

Olympic Champion

The all-around title is the most prestigious in gymnastics. American Paul Hamm was one of the favorites to win that title at the 2004 Olympic Games in Athens, Greece. But his hopes for gold faded when he fell on his landing in the vault competition. The vault is one of six events in the men's all-around. Hamm's mistake dropped him to twelfth in the all-around standings with two events left.

"I thought, "That's it. I'm done,'" Hamm said. "Maybe I had a small chance of winning a bronze medal [for third]."

His coach tried to lift his spirits. He told Hamm that he could still win gold by scoring at least 9.8 on each of the final two events. Hamm had not earned such a high score in any of the events he had competed in the Olympic Games to that point. But he was strong in his final two events.

Paul Hamm of the United States, *center*, won the coveted all-around gold medal at the 2004 Olympic Games in Athens, Greece.

Alan Kulwicki poses at Times Square in New York City after winning the 1992 Cup Series.

Hamm first went to the parallel bars. He was fantastic. Hamm scored a 9.837. He still had a chance, but it remained slim. Meanwhile, other competitors made mistakes. With one event left, Hamm was fourth.

His final event was the horizontal bar. "If he could pull a medal out of this, it would be an amazing comeback," the TV announcer said as Hamm began his routine. It began with Hamm swinging all the way around on the bar, first with both hands and then holding on with only one hand. Soon he was flying through the air like a bird on three consecutive release moves. He ended with a high-flying dismount and a stuck landing. When his spectacular performance ended, his coach yelled, "You're Olympic champion!"

Indeed he was. Hamm scored a 9.837. He became the first American to win the gold medal in the Olympic men's all-around competition. He won the gold medal by .012 of a point. It was the thinnest margin of victory ever in Olympic men's gymnastics.

"This is the greatest comeback in the history of gymnastics," former US gymnast Peter Vidmar told *Sports Illustrated* after Hamm's remarkable rally.

A Major Comeback

Johnny Miller didn't have a chance. After shooting a 76 in the third round of the 1973 US Open, he went into the final round in twelfth place, six strokes out of first place. To win, he would have to surpass some of the

Johnny Miller celebrates after sinking his final putt at the 1973 US Open in Oakmont, Pennsylvania.

sport's all-time greats, including Arnold Palmer, Jack Nicklaus, and Lee Trevino. And not only that, he would have to do it at Oakmont Country Club in Pennsylvania, where Palmer enjoyed strong support from his home state fans.

"I had no idea and no feeling that I had any chance whatsoever," Miller said.

Then the birds began to sing. Miller made birdies on the first four holes before making par on the next three. After a bogey, he ended the front nine with another birdie. Just like that, he was 4-under par for the round with nine holes to go.

Miller was never worse than par on the back nine. And with four birdies mixed in, he was better than the entire field in the four-round tournament. Miller's final round score of 63 was the lowest in US Open history (though it has since been matched). At 5-under-par 279, Miller took a one-stroke victory over John Schlee.

"It was the greatest round of golf in my life by a country mile," Miller said.

FUN FACTS

★ The European team of golfers needed to score eight out of 12 possible points on the final day of the 2012 Ryder Cup to win the tournament against American golfers. That's what the Europe team did in the semi-annual tournament to complete the remarkable comeback.

★ South Dearborn High School set the Indiana high school boys' basketball state record with the biggest fourth-quarter comeback. Trailing by 29, South Dearborn scored the final 30 points to beat East Central, 55–54.

★ Top-rated University of Illinois trailed third-ranked University of Arizona by 15 points with four minutes to go in their 2005 Elite 8 game. Illinois rallied and tied the game in regulation and won it in overtime 90–89 to advance to the Final Four.

★ In 2001, top-ranked Duke trailed Maryland by 22 points in the first half before rallying to win 95–84 to advance to the college basketball national championship game.

★ Nick Faldo trailed Greg Norman, ranked number one in the world at the time, by six strokes entering the final day of the 1996 Masters. Norman lost the tournament by five strokes when he shot a 78 to Faldo's final round 67.

★ John Tyler High School led Plano East in a 1994 Texas high school football playoff game 41–17 with a little more than three minutes left. Plano East scored four touchdowns to lead 44–41 with 24 seconds left before John Tyler returned the ensuring kickoff for a 97-yard touchdown to give John Tyler the 48–44 win.

GLOSSARY

ARCHRIVAL
An opponent that brings out the most passion in another opponent and its fans.

DRAFT
A system used in professional sports to disperse incoming talent among every team.

LATERALS
Passes in a football game that are thrown either sideways or backward.

LORE
Information that is passed down through the ages.

ONSIDE KICK
A play in football where the kicking team boots the ball a short distance in hopes of recovering the ball and keeping the other team from possessing it.

OVERTIME
An extra session of play if a contest remains tied after regulation.

STATUE OF LIBERTY PLAY
A trick play in football where the ball carrier takes the ball from the quarterback who is standing as if to make a pass.

TENDON
A flexible cord that attaches a muscle to a bone.

TWO-POINT CONVERSION
After a team scores a touchdown in a football game, it can choose to kick an extra point or line up and try to make it to the end zone from the 3-yard line (college) or 2-yard line (NFL) to score two points.

WILD CARD
Playoff berths given to the best remaining teams that did not win their respective divisions.

FOR MORE INFORMATION

Selected Bibliography

Bradley, Richard. *The Greatest Game: The Yankees, the Red Sox and the Playoff of '78*. New York: Free Press, a division of Simon & Schuster, 2008.

Chansky, Art. *The Dean's List: A Celebration of Tar Heel Basketball and Dean Smith*. New York: Warner Books, 1996.

Lucas, Adam. *Carolina Basketball: A Century of Excellence*. Chapel Hill, N.C: University of North Carolina Press, 2010.

Menzer, Joe. *Four Corners: How UNC, N.C. State, Duke and Wake Forest Made North Carolina the Center of the Basketball Universe*. New York: Simon & Schuster, 1999.

Shaughnessy, Dan. *Reversing the Curse: Inside the 2004 Boston Red Sox*. New York: Houghton Mifflin Harcourt, 2005.

Warner, Kurt, with Michael Silver. *All Things Possible: My Story of Faith, Football, and the Miracle Season*. San Francisco: HarperCollins Publishers, 2000.

Further Readings

Bay Area News Group. *Comeback Kings: The San Francisco Giants' Incredible 2012 Championship Season*. Chicago, IL: Triumph Books, 2012.

Noyes, Richard J., and Pamela J. Robertson. *Guts in the Clutch: 77 Legendary Triumphs, Heartbreaks, and Wild Finishes in 12 Sports*. Charleston, SC: BookSurge Publishing, 2009.

Sarkett, John A. *Extraordinary Comebacks SPORTS: Stories of Courage, Triumph, and Success*. Naperville, IL: CreateSpace Independent Publishing Platform, 2012.

Wilner, Barry, and Ken Rappoport. *Harvard Beats Yale 29-29 . . . and Other Great Comebacks from the Annals of Sports*. Lanham, MD: Taylor Trade Publishing, 2007.

Web Links

To learn more about the greatest comebacks in sports, visit ABDO Publishing Company online at **www.abdopublishing.com**. Web sites about the greatest comebacks in sports are featured on our Book Links page. These links are routinely monitored and updated to provide the most current information available.

Places to Visit

Naismith Memorial Basketball Hall of Fame
1000 Hall Fame Ave
Springfield, MA 01105
(413) 781-6500
www.hoophall.com
The Naismith Memorial Basketball Hall of Fame honors basketball's greatest players and moments.

National Baseball Hall of Fame and Museum
25 Main Street
Cooperstown, NY 13326
(888) 425-5633
www.baseballhall.org
This hall of fame and museum highlights the greatest players and moments in the history of baseball.

Pro Football Hall of Fame
2121 George Halas Drive NW
Canton, OH 44708
(330) 456-8207
www.profootballhof.com
This hall of fame and museum highlights the greatest players and moments in the history of the NFL.

INDEX

About the Author

Dustin Long is an award-winning journalist who has covered sports since 1985. His work has appeared in the *New York Times*, *USA Today*, SI.com, and in newspapers in Idaho, Indiana, North Carolina, Virginia, and Maryland. He authored *The Petty Family Album: In Tribute to Adam Petty* and *Daytona 500*. Raised in Indiana, he lives near Charlotte, North Carolina, with his wife.